Action Origami

Joe Fullman

Gareth Stevens
PUBLISHING

Please visit our website, www.garethstevens.com. For a free color catalog of all our high-quality books, call toll free 1-800-542-2595 or fax 1-877-542-2596.

Cataloging-in-Publication Data

Fullman, Joe.
Action origami / by Joe Fullman.
p. cm. — (Amazing origami)
Includes index.
ISBN 978-1-4824-4169-7 (pbk.)
ISBN 978-1-4824-4170-3 (6-pack)
ISBN 978-1-4824-4173-4 (library binding)
1. Origami — Juvenile literature. 2. Paper work — Juvenile literature.
I. Fullman, Joe. II. Title.
TT870.F85 2016
736'.982—d23

First Edition

Published in 2016 by
Gareth Stevens Publishing
111 East 14th Street, Suite 349
New York, NY 10003

Models and photography: Belinda Webster and Michael Wiles
Text: Joe Fullman
Design: Emma Randall
Editor: Frances Evans

Printed in the United States of America

CPSIA compliance information: Batch CW16GS: For further information contact Gareth Stevens, New York, New York at 1-800-542-2595.

Contents

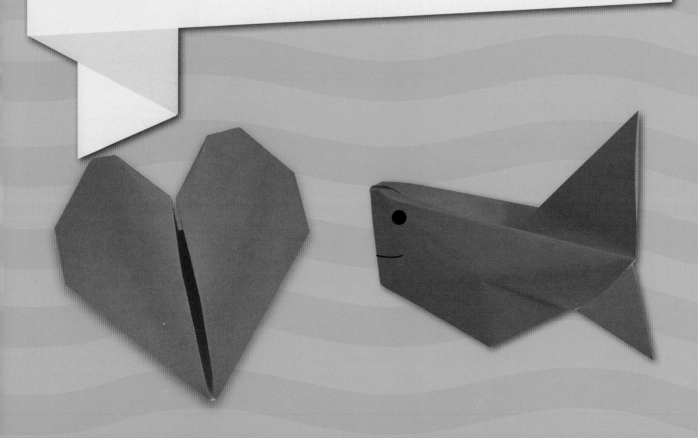

Basic Folds

Origami has been popular in Japan for hundreds of years and is now loved all around the world. You can make great models with just one sheet of paper... and this book shows you how!

The paper used in origami is thin but strong, so that it can be folded many times. It is usually colored on one side. Alternatively you can use ordinary scrap paper, but make sure it's not too thick.

Origami models often share the same folds and basic designs. This introduction explains some of the folds that you will need for the projects in this book, and they will also come in useful if you make other origami models. When making the models in this book, follow the key below to find out what the lines and arrows mean. And always crease well!

KEY

valley fold ------------

mountain fold ················

step fold (mountain and valley fold next to each other)

direction to move paper

push

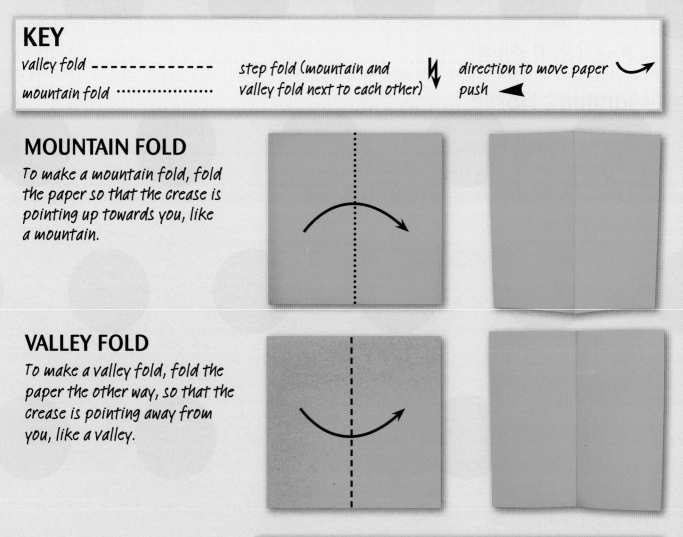

MOUNTAIN FOLD

To make a mountain fold, fold the paper so that the crease is pointing up towards you, like a mountain.

VALLEY FOLD

To make a valley fold, fold the paper the other way, so that the crease is pointing away from you, like a valley.

A NOTE ABOUT MEASUREMENTS

Measurements are given in U.S. form with the metric in parentheses. The metric conversion is rounded to make it easier to measure.

INSIDE REVERSE FOLD

An inside reverse fold is useful if you want to make a nose or a tail, or if you want to flatten off the shape of another part of an origami model.

1 Practice by first folding a piece of paper diagonally in half. Make a valley fold on one point and crease.

2 It's important to make sure that the paper is creased well. Run your finger over the crease two or three times.

3 Unfold and open up the corner slightly. Refold the crease nearest to you into a mountain fold.

open

4 Open up the paper a little more and then tuck the tip of the point inside. Close the paper. This is the view from the underside of the paper.

5 Flatten the paper. You now have an inside reverse fold.

OUTSIDE REVERSE FOLD

An outside reverse fold is useful if you want to make a head, beak or foot, or another part of your model that sticks out.

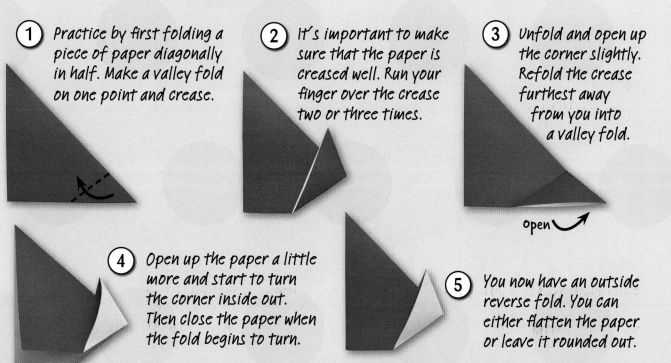

1 Practice by first folding a piece of paper diagonally in half. Make a valley fold on one point and crease.

2 It's important to make sure that the paper is creased well. Run your finger over the crease two or three times.

3 Unfold and open up the corner slightly. Refold the crease furthest away from you into a valley fold.

open

4 Open up the paper a little more and start to turn the corner inside out. Then close the paper when the fold begins to turn.

5 You now have an outside reverse fold. You can either flatten the paper or leave it rounded out.

5

Windmill

Attach your origami windmill to a stick, take it outside and watch it go round and round as the breeze catches it.

① Place your paper white side up with a straight edge facing you. Valley fold in half from right to left, then unfold.

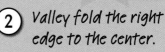

② Valley fold the right edge to the center.

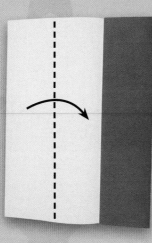

③ Valley fold the left edge to the center.

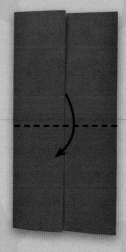

④ Valley fold the paper in half from top to bottom, then unfold.

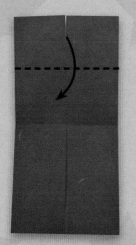

⑤ Valley fold the top edge to the center line.

⑥ Valley fold the bottom edge to the center line.

7 Your paper should look like this. Unfold the folds you made in steps 5 and 6.

8 Your paper should now be divided into eight small squares. Open up the top right-hand side.

9 With the top right side open, make a diagonal fold across the small square second from the top on the right, like this.

10 Repeat steps 8 and 9 on the left-hand side, then fold the top edge forwards.

11 Your paper should look like this. Flatten the top part down.

12 Repeat steps 8, 9, 10 and 11 on the bottom half of the paper.

13 Diagonally fold the top right-hand corner up to the top.

14 Now diagonally fold the bottom left-hand corner down to the bottom.

Open

Open

Open

Open

15 Open up each of the four points slightly.

Spinning Around

To spin properly, you need to attach the windmill to something – a stick or pencil with an unfolded paper clip attached to one end works well. Simply insert one end of the paper clip through the center of the windmill to hold it in place – ask an adult to help. A blob of sticky tack at the end of the paper clip will stop the windmill from spinning off.

16 Your windmill is ready to spin in the wind!

Inflatable Goldfish

Goldfish are popular pets. Follow these instructions to make your own origami version. This one also comes with a special surprise – it expands when you blow into it!

1. Place your paper colored side up with a straight edge facing you. Valley fold in half from top to bottom, and unfold. Then valley fold in half from left to right, and unfold.

2. Turn your paper over from left to right.

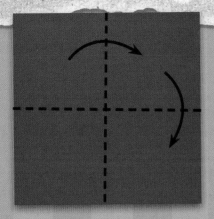

Push ►   ◄ Push

3. Make a diagonal valley fold from the top left corner to the bottom right, and unfold. Then diagonally valley fold the top right corner down to the bottom left, and unfold.

4. Push the left and right edges of your paper in towards each other.

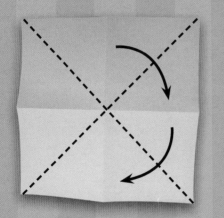

Push

5. The paper should start to fold in on itself.

6. Keep pushing so the paper forms a triangle. Press it flat.

7. On the top layer, valley fold the bottom right corner up to the top.

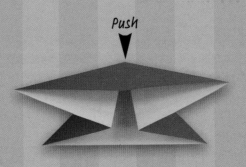

8 Repeat step 7 on the left-hand side.

9 On the top layer, fold the middle right point to the center line.

10 Repeat step 9 on the left-hand side.

11 On the top layer, fold the top right point down to meet the fold made in step 9.

12 Repeat step 11 on the left-hand side.

13 Tuck the fold you made in step 11 into the fold you made in step 9.

Tuck

Push

14 Keep pushing until the fold is all the way in.

Push

15 Repeat steps 13 and 14 on the left-hand side.

Did You Know?

The world's oldest pet goldfish, Tish, lived for 43 years. He was won as a prize at a fair in 1956 and died in 1999.

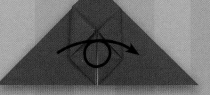

16 Your paper should look like this. Turn it over from left to right.

17 Fold the right point over to the center line.

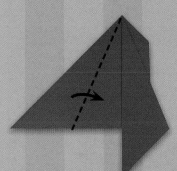

18 Repeat Step 17 on the left-hand side.

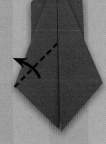

19 Valley fold the bottom left point over to the left, as shown.

20 Fold the entire left-hand flap over to the right.

21 Flatten the paper down

Blow

22 To inflate your goldfish, carefully blow into the area circled here.

23 Your goldfish is ready. Why not make him a few more friends to play with? They can be any color you like!

Beating Heart

This is a romantic origami heart with a difference – it really beats! With a bit of practice, you should be able to make it beat really fast.

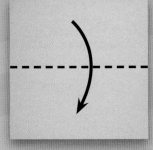

1. Place your paper white side up with a straight edge facing you. Valley fold it in half from top to bottom, then unfold.

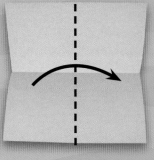

2. Valley fold the paper in half from left to right.

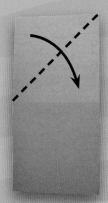

3. Valley fold the top left corner down to the center line.

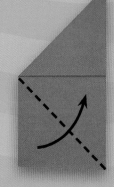

4. Now fold the bottom left corner up to the center line.

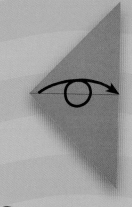

5. Turn the paper over from left to right.

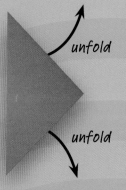

6. Unfold the folds you made in steps 3 and 4.

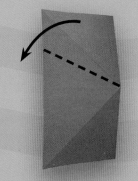

7. Make a diagonal valley fold in the top half, bringing the top left point down and to the left.

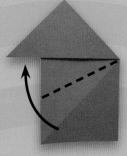

8. Repeat on the bottom half, making a diagonal fold and bringing the bottom left point up and to the left.

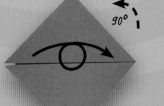

9 Your paper should look like this. Turn it 90° counterclockwise, then turn it over from left to right.

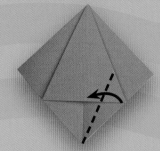

10 Your paper should look like this. Make a small diagonal valley fold on the right side, as shown.

11 Make a small diagonal valley fold on the left-hand side, as shown.

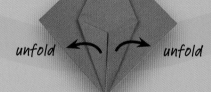

12 Open up the folds you made in steps 10 and 11.

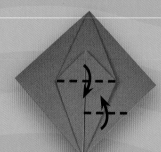

13 Start opening up the horizontal flap, as shown.

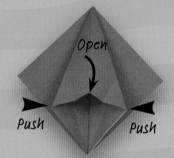

14 As you open the horizontal flap, start pushing the two edges on either side together.

15 As the two sides come together, they'll form a triangular shape at the top. Push this up and flatten it down.

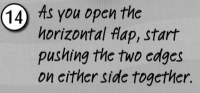

16 Your paper should look like this. Valley fold the central point forwards so it's standing upright. This will be the handle. Then valley fold the bottom right point to the center.

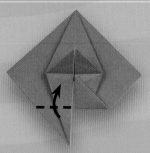

17 Valley fold the bottom left point to the center.

18 Diagonally valley fold the bottom right center point to meet the edge of the fold you made in step 16.

19 Diagonally valley fold the bottom left center point to meet the edge of the fold you made in step 17.

20 Your paper should look like this. Rotate it 180°.

Tuck

Tuck

Tuck

21 Take the top right flap and start to tuck it behind the central folds of the paper.

22 Keep tucking until most of the flap is out of sight.

23 Now repeat steps 21 and 22 on the left-hand side.

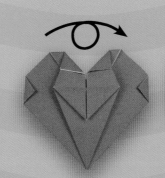

24 Your paper should look like this. Make small, equal-sized valley folds on the left- and right-hand sides.

25 Turn the paper over and your heart is ready.

26 Hold the handle between your thumb and first two fingers and push them forward to make the heart beat.

Pop-Up Rabbit

Wish someone a "Hoppy Birthday" with this amazing pop-up bunny card. It might take a bit of practice to get it to pop just right.

1 Place the paper white side up with a straight edge facing you. Valley fold it in half from left to right, then unfold.

2 Valley fold the right edge to the center line.

3 Valley fold the left edge to the center line.

4 Fold the top right corner down to the center line, as shown.

5 Fold the top left corner down to the center line.

6 Open up the folds you made in steps 4 and 5.

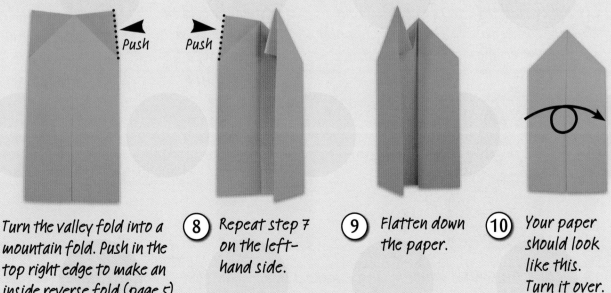

Push

Push

7 Turn the valley fold into a mountain fold. Push in the top right edge to make an inside reverse fold (page 5).

8 Repeat step 7 on the left-hand side.

9 Flatten down the paper.

10 Your paper should look like this. Turn it over.

Did You Know?

Rabbits have very strong back legs, which allow them to jump more than 9.8 ft (3 m) to escape from a predator.

(11) On the top layer, valley fold down the top point.

(12) Turn the paper over from left to right.

(13) Valley fold the right corner to the center line.

(14) Valley fold the left corner to the center line.

(15) Valley fold the top point forwards.

(16) Valley fold the point up again, forming a 1/3-inch (1cm) step.

(17) Your paper should look like this. Turn it over from left to right.

Tuck

(18) Untuck the central point so it's in front of the horizontal edge.

(19) Make a small valley fold just above the edge.

(20) Valley fold the paper in half.

21 On the top layer, valley fold the top point to the right, as shown, to form the first ear.

22 Your paper should look like this. Repeat step 21 on the other side.

23 Untuck the folds in between the ears, and pull the paper out to the left to form the head.

Push

Push

24 Push the central horizontal folds up, and flatten the folds out to push the rabbit's head backwards. Be sure to do this on both sides at the same time.

25 Fold the top ear forwards, as shown.

Push

Open

26 Repeat step 25 with the other ear.

Close

Push

Close

27 Push the head backwards and down, while opening out the rectangular shapes at the bottom.

28 Your paper should look like this. Press the face down and close the card until it's flat.

Open

29 Your paper should look like this – just like a flat card. But open it up quickly and the rabbit will pop out!

30 Say hello to the pop-up rabbit.

Jumping Horse

Whoa there! This leaping origami horse will perform forward somersaults right before your very eyes. You'll need scissors to complete your model, so get an adult to help you.

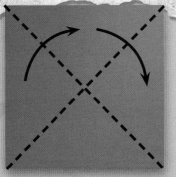

1 Place your paper colored side up with a straight edge facing you. Valley fold the paper in half diagonally both ways, then unfold.

2 Your paper should look like this. Turn it over.

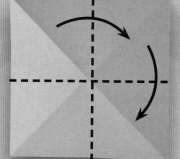

3 Valley fold the paper in half from top to bottom, and unfold. Then valley fold it in half from left to right, and unfold.

4 Rotate the paper, so that a corner is facing you. Then push the two outer edges in towards each other.

5 As you push, the paper should start folding up into a small square, like this. Flatten it down.

6 Valley fold the right corner of the top layer over to the center line.

7 Valley fold the left corner of the top layer over to the center line.

8 Valley fold the top point down, as shown.

9 Open up the folds you made in steps 6, 7 and 8.

10 Now, use scissors to make a straight cut in the top layer only, from the bottom point to the top horizontal fold.

Cut

11 Your paper should look like this. Valley fold the top layer up to the top on both the left and right sides.

12 Your paper should look like this. Valley fold the left center point of the top layer over to the center line. Then do the same on the right-hand side.

13 Your paper should look like this. Turn it over from left to right, and then repeat steps 6 to 12 on the other side.

Did You Know?

Horses are able to run and jump shortly after being born.

14 Your paper should look like this. Rotate it 180°.

180°

15 Valley fold the top right point over to the right, as shown.

16 Now valley fold the right point the other way, so it's also a mountain fold. Then turn it into an inside reverse fold (see page 5). This is your horse's tail.

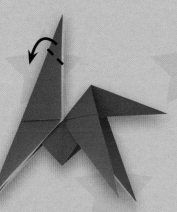

17 Make a valley fold near the top of the top left point, as shown.

18 Now valley fold it the other way, so it's also a mountain fold. Then turn it into an inside reverse fold (see page 5). This is your horse's head.

19 Start forming a nose by making a small valley fold at the end of the head.

20 Valley fold it the other way, so it's also a mountain fold. Then turn it into an inside reverse fold (see page 5). Your horse is ready to perform!

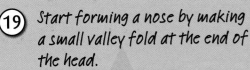

21 To make him jump, flick his tail hard up in the air and he should perform a forward somersault – and land on his feet!

Egg-Laying Hen

Cluck, cluck! With just a single piece of paper you can make both a hen and a little egg. You'll need some scissors for the final stage, so get an adult to help you.

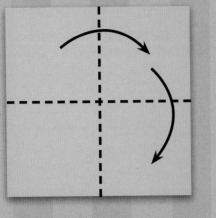

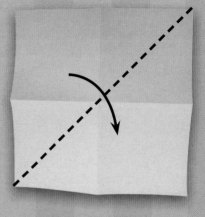

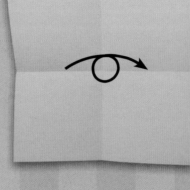

① Place your paper colored side up with a straight edge facing you. Valley fold in half from top to bottom, and unfold. Then valley fold in half from left to right, and unfold.

② Turn your paper over.

③ Diagonally valley fold the top left corner to the bottom right, and unfold.

Push

Push

180°

④ Turn your paper so the diagonal fold you made in step 3 is now horizontal and a corner is facing you. Start pressing the left- and right-hand sides together.

⑤ As you press, the paper should start to fold up into a small square, like this. Flatten it down.

⑥ Your paper should look like this. Rotate it 180°, so the open end is at the top.

Did You Know?

The chicken is the most common bird in the world. There are around 50 billion of them – or about seven for every human. That's a lot of eggs!

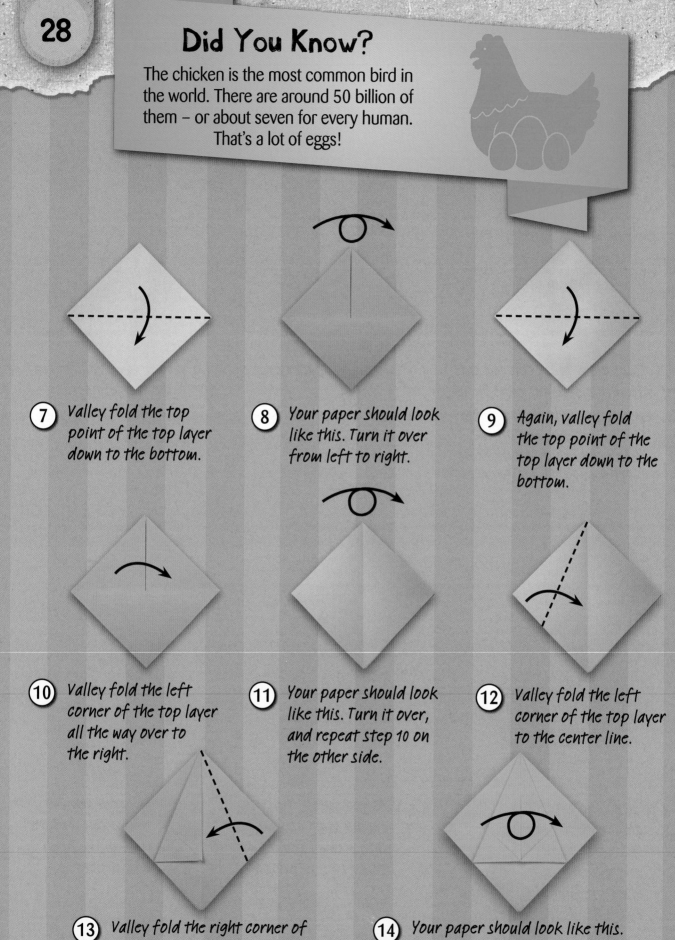

7 Valley fold the top point of the top layer down to the bottom.

8 Your paper should look like this. Turn it over from left to right.

9 Again, valley fold the top point of the top layer down to the bottom.

10 Valley fold the left corner of the top layer all the way over to the right.

11 Your paper should look like this. Turn it over, and repeat step 10 on the other side.

12 Valley fold the left corner of the top layer to the center line.

13 Valley fold the right corner of the top layer to the center line.

14 Your paper should look like this. Turn it over from left to right.

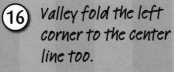

15 Valley fold the right corner to the center line.

16 Valley fold the left corner to the center line too.

17 Your paper should look like this.

18 Fold the left flap all the way over to the right.

19 Turn the paper over from left to right, then again fold the left flap all the way to the right.

20 Your paper should look like this with a clear gap between the top two points. To start making the tail, make a diagonal valley fold in the top right point, as shown.

21 Now fold the top right point back the other way, so it's also a mountain fold. Then turn it into an inside reverse fold (see page 5).

22 Open the right side up a little. Then mountain fold the tip of the tail downwards, and tuck it under.

23 Your paper should look like this. Flatten it down.

24 Start to make the head by valley folding the left point over to the left, as shown.

25 Now fold the point the other way, so it's also a mountain fold, then turn it into an inside reverse fold (see page 5).

26 Your paper should look like this. Make another, smaller inside reverse fold going the other way (see page 5).

27 Make a final inside reverse fold going back the other way to form the beak.

28 Your paper should look like this. Valley fold the bottom point of the top layer up, as shown.

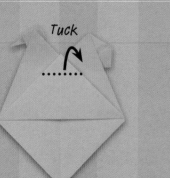
Tuck

29 Tuck the point behind the middle flap.

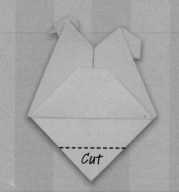
Cut

30 Take your scissors and make a horizontal cut through the paper about 3/4 in (2 cm) from the bottom.

31 You'll be left with two pieces of paper, like this.

Tuck

(32) Take the smaller piece of paper and mountain fold the right point of the top layer behind.

(33) Tuck the flap behind. Then repeat on the left-hand side.

(34) Your paper should look like this. Turn it over from left to right and repeat steps 32 and 33 on the other side.

(35) Your smaller piece of paper should look like this. This is the egg.

(36) Slide the egg into the top of your paper. Move the side flaps up and down and watch the egg pop out the bottom. It looks like your hen has laid its first egg!

Glossary

crease A line in a piece of paper made by creasing.

expand To become bigger in size or amount.

inflate To fill something with gas or air so that it swells up.

mountain fold An origami step where a piece of paper is folded so that the crease is pointing upward, like a mountain.

predator An animal that eats other animals.

somersault An acrobatic movement in which a person turns head over heels in the air or on the ground.

step fold A mountain fold and valley fold next to each other.

sticky tack A type of putty that can be used to attach light objects to walls or dry surfaces.

valley fold An origami step where a piece of paper is folded so that the crease is pointing downwards, like a valley.

Further Reading

Akass, Susan. *My First Origami Book*. Cico Kidz, 2011.

Robinson, Nick. *The Awesome Origami Pack*. Barron's Educational Series, Inc., 2014.

Robinson, Nick. *World's Best Origami*. New York: Alpha Books, 2010.

Index